THE STORYTELLING METHOD

STEPS TO MAXIMIZE A SIMPLE STORY AND MAKE IT POWERFUL, INSPIRING, AND UNFORGETTABLE

MATT MORRIS

CONTENTS

Introduction   v

1. Storytelling   1
2. 10 Steps to Telling a Story   6
3. Use of Metaphors   13
4. How To Talk To Anyone   17
5. Types of Stories To Tell   23
6. Final Tips to Becoming a Master Storyteller   29

Afterword   31

INTRODUCTION

Let's say you're in a group of 5 people. One is Mr. Social who always has something to say; next is The Nice Guy who pretty much agrees with everything anybody says; then there's The Drama Queen who always is up to date on the latest gossip, and if there's nothing new, then she'll create something new! And we can't forget about the guy's guy who is always up to date on the latest sports news and is practically a beer snob...

And then there's you, who has the ability to take over the conversation and lead it in any direction you choose. You're the person who knows what to say and when to say it. You're the person who can take something that happened yesterday, or an hour ago, or a year ago, and spin it into something entertaining and visually intriguing - a compelling story that people are dying to hear about. You understand what a story needs.

This is you after you're done reading and implementing the strategies in this Storytelling book. Let's get started!

STORYTELLING

The ability to tell a story is one of the most powerful skills anybody can have. I'm not just talking any story, but I am talking about the ability to take a simple story and turn it around so it becomes captivating, enticing, and leaves the listener either bursting with laughter, feeling on top of the world so that he can go out and accomplish anything, or completely leaving someone in awe, on the verge of tears at how powerful and how much your story touched the listener.

THE LISTENER COULD BE someone you just met at a coffee shop that you were drawn to, or it could be your neighbor, or an auditorium packed with listeners waiting to be inspired, or your children as you're tucking them in bed.

THESE ARE the skills a natural storyteller has; at the same time, the great news is that ANYONE can become a natural storyteller given the proper tools and strategies (which you're reading now), and willingness to get into action and improve the skill of storytelling.

Stories are used in every setting, all around the world. They are the backbone to all new relationships, spreading the word about all great new ideas, and keeping listeners entertained.

What Is Storytelling & Why Is It Important?

I'll give you a brief background on storytelling and its uses before we jump into the methods of how to make a story powerful, inspiring, and unforgettable. The art of storytelling has been around since the beginning of mankind. It can be defined as an ancient art form that allows people to actively express thoughts and ideas in an interactive way that stimulates the imagination of the listener. When Jesus was roaming the earth, he used powerful stories to inspire disciples to follow him and, in turn, impacted millions of lives for centuries. How powerful do you want your stories to be?

Storytelling is a two way street - You've got the storyteller and the listener. The listener's response to the storyteller often dictates the teller's next move, depending on what type of a response he wants. For example, a good comedian listens to the response of the audience to determine which direction he wants to go next. Does he want more laughter? Does he want an emotional response? Does he want them to be shocked? Whatever type of response he wants, he has the ability to get it by reading and listening to the impact of the story on the audience.

Storytellers use both spoken language and body language

to express the events and characters in the story often through physical movement and vocalization.

Presenting A Story

When a storyteller can relate a story to the audience, it causes listeners' ears to perk up. The main idea of storytelling is to relate a story. For example, everybody has errands to run from time to time. Maybe you went to the store to grab some milk and someone's dog in the check out line wouldn't stop sniffing you. Well, people can relate in many ways to this simple story. For instance, everyone has gone to the grocery store, and most people have bought milk before, and I'd imagine some people have been sniffed by a dog (not always in a grocery store). The point is that we can all find a way to relate to practically EVERY story!

Stroking the imagination is key when portraying certain events and characters to the listener. Get descriptive, messy, and specific. The more realistic you can paint the picture, the more likely the reader will listen and remember the story. If the dog sniffing you was gross, how gross was it? Did it remind you of something? What did it feel like when you were being sniffed? Adding these details would add to the juiciness behind it all. One of the most important roles of a storyteller is to stimulate creativity by using vivid imagery.

The interesting thing is that no one person will ever have the exact same images as another person – because clearly no two people have the exact same imagination. It's like you're co-creating and designing the story together. While you're telling the story, you can guide the listener to design and feel whatever you want.

Why Is It Important?

For many years, humans have relied on storytelling to pass their traditions, and share family past-times. Nowadays, the method for storytelling has drastically changed. Today, if you want to reach a larger audience quickly, you can film yourself straight from home and put it on YouTube or Vimeo.com, and your story could be spread across the world in a matter of days. On a smaller scale, you can tell a story to your co-worker, or your child just before bed and each will have a different impact. Below I'll list a few examples of where storytelling is used and for what purpose.

Cultural Interaction

Exchanging different stories from city to city and country to country can be great way to open one's mind and learn more about other cultures. This method can teach both children and adults a lot of things about the world. The stories can push people to want to go see Africa, for example, or can totally scare them and steer them away from getting anywhere near Africa. It depends on what kind of an impact you want your stories to have on the listener.

Storytelling can highlight positive and negative consequences in life. People will also be familiar with their own tradition as well as the custom and personalities of other people.

Social Experience

Storytelling has always been a primary form of entertainment. It can provide a fun experience for both children and adults. People can be so caught up in a story that, before you know it, the person is laughing hysterically, or you glance at the listener and they have an extremely annoyed look in their eyes. Stories can and will elicit emotional responses and are excellent ways to break the ice and immediately connect with one another.

To Teach a Lesson

Often, stories uncover a gem or life lesson that will only be revealed at the end of the story. With a story, you can take something mundane (such as filing paperwork) and turn it into a beautiful work of art (when you were filing paperwork, and all of a sudden you realized something incredible about yourself).

As you're telling your story, the listener will be influenced by your words, rhythm and tone. You'll come to realize which elements make the stories more interesting and exciting. This knowledge will enable you to improve and highlight certain aspects of the story each time you retell it.

Let's go ahead and jump into what's important here – the steps to telling a good story.

10 STEPS TO TELLING A STORY

Throughout human history, the greatest leaders, teachers, and entertainers have used stories to communicate a particular message. Storytelling requires you to use different skills to engage the audience and draw them into your stories.

Here are the basic steps that can help you turn a simple story into something powerful and unforgettable.

1. Get a story

If you don't already have a story, or at least something in mind that you want to expand upon, then go grab a pen and piece of paper and let's get you unstuck with some quick brainstorming.

On the paper, write 5 categories: Who, What, When, Where, and Why. Then fill in the blanks to one or all of these questions:

- If I could do anything right in this very moment, I would_____

- If I could travel anywhere tomorrow, I would go to_____
- The thing that makes me laugh most is _____
- To me, TV is _____
- When I was (pick the first number that comes to your head), I thought a lot about _____.
- Today I learned _____.

Next, answer the 5 category questions to assist in creating a story (e.g. Who was there?)

These are a few examples of things that will get you started with creating and telling stories. If you already have your own brainstorming style, then of course you can go ahead and do that.

2. Enjoy Your Story

You, the storyteller must enjoy what you're talking about. Therefore, be sure you've chosen a story that's interesting, funny, has a lesson behind it, etc.

It is key to have fun with the story and play around with its details – maybe add a touch of sarcasm or lightheartedness. See how it makes you feel as you imagine yourself telling it.

If it provokes the emotional impact you want, then go ahead and keep it as is, only slightly adjusting to each listener. If it doesn't work, throw out the detail you just added and try something new. The key is to play around and have fun with it, because the more enjoyable it is for you, the more enjoyable and entertaining it'll be for your listener.

Aside from enjoying the story, you should also be able to understand the whole story enough that you don't need any cue cards. This will make the process sound more spontaneous and fun. Know how the story starts and how it ends. If you must create changes, do it in the middle of the story.

3. Add Emotion

One of the best ways to tell a story is to add emotion to it. I must admit that it's generally easier for women to do this than men. But men, if you want your stories to be impactful and unforgettable (especially to women) then you must add some emotion - whether it be heartbreaking or the funniest thing you've ever seen! If you cannot add any emotion to the story, the listener will have trouble relating to the story. Here are some tips that can help you add emotions to your stories.

First, close your eyes and try to relive that moment in your life. Actually see yourself doing it or being there as if you were a bird watching from a tree. Visualize and re-experience it completely in your mind.

While doing this, you should be able to conjure strong emotions that you can use in storytelling. When you tell it, relive the emotions as if you're re-experiencing it. The listener will be able to hear your emotions in your voice, so the more you can feel the emotion while telling it, the more engaging it will be. Be passionate about the story to elicit a greater response from the audience.

Keep in mind that when you're trying to inject emotion in a story, try not to overdo it or make it "overdramatic," or your listener will be exhausted just from listening to you. Maybe rehearse it with a close friend to help you gauge your emotional range before telling it to people you don't know as well. Again, it depends on what kind of an impact you want to have and to whom you are telling the story. Will you be telling it to a stranger in the mall, or your boss at work, or your spouse, or a group of college students via YouTube?

. . .

4. Add Pauses

Every good storyteller knows that a pause can do so many things. It can heighten the tension of the scene, or simply allow the audience to absorb the information given to them, or give the listener an opportunity to laugh or respond back with a "Really?" "Oh my gosh" or "No way!"

As you're creating your story, think through where you'd want pauses. Try to put yourself in the listener's shoes - if you were the listener and you were being told your story, where would you want pauses?

Where would you need time to think and process what's going on?

Where would you be curious or feel suspense about what's going to happen next?

Add pauses there to hike up the intensity.

5. Use Body Language

Emotions can be translated through body language. Be aware of how you are standing when you're telling the story. How's your posture? Are you standing straight up and confident or serious; are you slumped over and looking depressed?

Take note of how much space you take up when telling your story - are your feet far apart or close together? Generally, men take up more space, which has been recognized as a sign of power and being confident. Are your hands and arms moving as you speak – if so, it can add emphasis. Be sure, though, that they are not moving too much and being a distraction from what you're saying.

Rehearse your story. You do not want to confuse the audience with your movements. A classic technique to master body language is by practicing in front of the mirror. Nowadays it's also common to use a video camera or a smart phone to record yourself, watch the video, and then make adjustments.

6. Use Your 5 Senses To Amplify The Story

The more visually descriptive you can make your story, the more entertaining it will be. Stories are best told if you can both feel and see the story unfolding. Words are powerful, so add visually descriptive adjectives to the story.

For example, if you're talking about a fruit you had for lunch, you could say, "Today I had the most delicious strawberries. As I bit into one, I could feel the juices squirting out," or "As I bit into the orange, it made a crunch sound and I was confused," or "When I first glanced at the perfectly pink peach with a hint of orange and the little fur coming off it, I knew I had to have it," or "I could smell the fresh pineapple from ten feet away, and I glanced over my shoulder and I saw the lady was giving away samples."

Ask yourself:
- How did it feel?
- How did it taste?
- What did it look like?
- What did it sound like?
- What did it smell like?

We will expand on this in the next Chapter, when we talk about metaphors and how powerful they can be.

7. Characterization

The characters in your story are just like real people. When describing them, give them their own personality and unique traits. Emphasize characters using emotions. A simple example would be Little Red Riding Hood, who was very naïve, and the wolf, who was cunning and sly. It adds to the story if you can change your tone of voice, rhythm, and even speed when describing each of the characters. And of course, you can rehearse the story a few times to become more confident with the characters' personas.

8. Know the audience

Are you telling your story to a bunch of kindergarteners? Are you telling it to a few coworkers over lunch? Are you telling it to a stranger in a bar? Think of to whom you are telling it, and try to predict their response and the response you'll receive. Visualization often helps with this. So, close your eyes for a moment and imagine being in the setting you want to share your story, and imagine going through the motions of telling your story. Now imagine the listener's response to your story. Was that the response you wanted? If not, take a moment to rehearse it in your mind until it flows the way you want it.

It is vital for any storyteller to relate a narrative to the appropriate audience. You're not going to be telling a bunch of kindergarteners about something that you might tell a coworker at lunch. You have to have an idea of how they will react to your story. Age, gender, professional level, and even religious views are important considerations in choosing a story. In addition, the language you use, and even the tone of voice you use must be taken into consideration. Remember that, even if you are telling a well-rehearsed old story, what might be funny for one group can be offensive for another.

If you're telling a story to a large group of people, the topic of the story should be broad enough for everyone to understand. This principle is also used in stand-up comedy. Comedians use mundane and everyday experiences to make their quips relatable to everybody (such as brushing their teeth, or going to the gas station). You will be able to know if you have chosen the right story through the reaction of the audience, and you can always make adjustments, whether it be with your vocal language, body language, or tone of voice.

A storyteller should always be aware of his audience's reaction and know how to keep the audience engaged and entertained throughout the story. No matter how well you have prepared for it, you can still encounter problems. You should be flexible and creative enough to have a back-up plan ready.

9. Make sure there is a point to your story

We've all heard stories that have been pointless but still kept us engaged and excited because of the person's body language and voice qualities. Afterward, we might be asking ourselves, what was the point of that story?

Stories are always best when the story has a bottom line or point, or comedic punch-line, or a lesson to be learned; if there is not point, the story might not be worth telling. People will usually look for the bottom line or purpose of why the story was told in the first place.

10. Write your story and cut it in half

Often, the storyteller gets too caught up in his or her own story and loses the listener's attention. As a general tip, write your story the way you want it and then cut it in half. Keep the KISS philosophy in mind. It stands for "Keep It Short and Simple (one of the many variations)". Try to leave only the most captivating and important parts(using the 5 senses rule of thumb) of the story - and nothing else. Some people emphasize too much detail that may be irrelevant to the story.

USE OF METAPHORS

Storytellers use a number of tools to enhance their stories and make them come to life. One of the best skills a storyteller can have is the use of metaphors, which are types of visual images. They allow the listener to immediately design a picture in his or her mind while expressing several things at once. Metaphors not only bring the stories to life, but the listener often feels as if he were there too.

One of the best things about metaphors is that they allow the audience to personally design and create pictures in their minds, and therefore the listeners will likely be more attentive and engaged because they're actively using their minds.

Types of metaphors

Metaphors are often used to compare two unrelated objects and find a similarity between them. This allows listeners to relate to an object or a person, bringing a new understanding to the story. In the following paragraphs, the most common types of metaphors will be listed, and you can choose which type to incorporate into your story to bring it to life.

1. Absolute metaphor

In an absolute metaphor, there is absolutely no correlation between the two objects being compared. For example, when you say, "Her heart is stone," you do not literally mean that her heart was transformed into a stone - rather, you can be describing her as unemotional or incapable of love.

2. Active metaphor

An active metaphor is commonly found in poetry and stories. It is used to provoke a particular thought in the audience. An active metaphor may be mistaken for an absolute metaphor, but in an active metaphor, there is still a slight correlation between the two objects, such as "You are my sunshine."

3. Complex metaphor

Complex metaphor is used in riddles. It is so complex that it is difficult to understand and decipher the real correlation between the two objects. For example, "shedding a light" may be taken literally as bringing light into a dark area but it can also be used as a metaphor. Shedding a light may also mean understanding a situation.

4. Compound metaphor

A compound metaphor uses adverbs and adjectives to excite listeners. Compound metaphors are also known as loose metaphors, which add descriptive words. An example could be, "He could feel the heat rising."

5. Extended metaphor

This takes a single metaphor and uses different ways to describe it. This type of metaphor is often used when a storyteller wants to create a memorable scenario. The meaning of an extended metaphor is not concealed, but it is very elaborate.

An example of extended metaphor would be from Emily Dickinson's poem, "Hope is the Thing with Feathers," where Dickinson compares the concept of hope with a bird.

6. Pataphor

A pataphor is an extreme form of metaphor that is used to express excitement. For example, "She swam with such grace that the water was left undisturbed by her tail." This pataphor describes a girl who swims as gracefully as a fish. Be cautious with this one, though, because it can also be very confusing and may lead the audience to wonder whether it is really a girl or a fish.

7. Simple metaphor

A simple metaphor uses a single description and is used to convey simple messages and ideas. The storyteller won't have to use any flamboyant words; instead he can state it in a straightforward way. An example would be, "Bob is a dog," or "The school is a prison."

8. Submerged

A submerged metaphor has a deep meaning and requires the audience to have more understanding of the subject. Storytellers should stay away from this metaphor unless they are addressing a specific audience that has enough knowledge on the subject such as, "John's thoughts were on the wing," meaning that he was on a plane.

When people hear a picture being described, they draw up their own unique images in their minds. Metaphors enable a storyteller to convey a vast amount of information and ideas without doing or saying too much. Stories are already powerful enough to elicit an emotional response from the audience, and when they are combined with images, the message of the story becomes magnified and strengthed. They synergize the words in a story, ending up with a beautiful image that will be remembered.

HOW TO TALK TO ANYONE

Stories are shared in every social setting. They bring people together and allow people to connect from all over the world – from a story on the Internet or virtual web meeting to the person you're sitting next to. They form relationships, strengthen existing relationships, and allow people to share their thoughts and experiences.

MEETING NEW PEOPLE

Maybe you want to make a new friend, or maybe you want to begin a new relationship and start dating more, or maybe you want to meet your neighbors, but feel awkward because you don't know how to open the conversation. In this chapter, I want to talk briefly about three different types of conversation openers, because opening or starting a conversation is the hardest part for 95% of people. I've conveniently titled them:

1. The "Excuse me, do you know what time it is?"

. . .

2. THE "WELL, THANK YOU!"

3. THE "WELL, HELLO THERE."

ONE THING I want to mention is that, when opening a conversation, body language and facial expressions are very important. A smile makes a person much more receptive to your approach. You don't have to be smiling the entire time, but 70% is a good amount to show that you're happy to be talking to the other person.

If you're more interested in that, I highly recommend taking a look at my book titled *The Power Of NLP*, where I go into details about body language - how feet can tell you whether a person is interested or not; how the movement of the eyes can determine whether a person is a visual, kinesthetic, or auditory thinker; and how to determine if a person is lying. Let's begin with examples of how to begin a conversation.

1. "Excuse me, do you know what time it is?"

This is a very indirect opener, and it opens (meaning the person will be receptive) 99.9% of the time. You make it seem completely like you have no intention of talking to the person other than that you want the time. It is a very soft and easy way to open any conversation.

After you ask the question, you need to immediately transition (or change the subject). A strategy I've used that has been very successful for me is to be very present and be observant (using your 5 senses) about something about the person you're talking to, or something in the environment (although, mention nothing about the physical appearance of the other person because it might come off as a pick-up).

For instance, you might notice that the person you just met looks or sounds like your brother, or even a friend you met years ago while taking a road trip across America. Notice something around you – how the air smells so fresh, or how cool the weather is today, or that the trees have been changing color so fast this season, or how sunny it is today, or be curious about the shirt the person is wearing or the handbag she's carrying. It is key to use and be aware of your 5 senses when interacting and meeting new people. I've noticed that it is great for establishing comfort and building rapport.

If you want to take it to a deeper level quickly (which is a more advanced skill), notice something about the energy they give off when talking with them, and then mention it to them. Really begin to pick up on the person's words, and be curious about what they are saying and how they are saying it, as well as the message behind the words. This can bring the conversation to a whole new level in a matter of minutes.

Then begin with one of the stories you have created. With time and practice, you'll be able to determine which kind of story (out of your new stash of stories) will fit best in the situation and base it off your mood and the other person's mood, too. You can decide to lighten the mood with a happy story, or build comfort by telling a rapport-building story. You can tell a humorous story (which often builds comfort very fast) to make the person smile and feel good, a thought-provoking story, which often makes the person curious about you, or a wide array of stories that you've created.

After a few minutes, you will feel a hook, or comfort and connection built in the conversation, and you can decide where to take the conversation. Keep in mind, you can use a wide array of indirect openers, but the "Excuse me, do you know what time it is?" will work 99.9% of the time.

2. "Well, Thank you!"

This opener revolves around compliments and gift giving. Everyone loves genuine compliments, and people love receiving gifts. I stress the word "genuine," because most of the time, people can see through a non-genuine compliment based on tone of voice and facial expressions.

If you spot someone you'd like to talk to, notice something about them (again, not about their physical appearance). Maybe you like the hat they are wearing or the eyeglasses they are sporting. It can be a number of things. Then, it is very important to immediately go talk to that person, because if you wait a minute, or even a few too many seconds, you'll begin to get anxious and talk yourself out of it.

Another one is gift-giving (which is classic for making friends with your neighbors and co-workers). Imagine your neighbor – who you've seen once or twice – were to ring your doorbell and surprise you with a homemade apple pie, and introduce himself (and his family) to you and your family. Imagine how good that would feel to actually know your neighbors and become friends. Too often in our generation, it seems like people get too busy to introduce themselves to the people who should be on the top of the priority list of "people to meet" - the neighbors!

Also, giving a co-worker a gift (which is sometimes against office policies – so check first) is appreciated too. It is a great way to build comfort and establish rapport. For instance, you could bring a coworker (or the entire office) a cake that you baked last night, or a cool new pen that you thought they would like, or surprise them with a soda from the vending machine when you went to buy yourself one. If you haven't already, I recommend just trying it and experiment a little just to see what happens. It's fun and exciting to step outside of your comfort-zone every once in a while. Then of course, with each of these experiments, you'll want to transition with stories that you've created. This will build rapport and establish rewarding and meaningful relationships.

3. "Well, hello there."

This is a more direct and flirty approach, and it will not open every time - maybe not even half the time - but it cuts to the chase and gets right to the point. This one can be considered more assertive and sometime even aggressive. If you're not comfortable being direct or stepping out of your comfort-zone, you can stick with the first two.

With "Well, hello there," this breaks the rule of not mentioning anything about physical appearance. With this, it's best if you notice something about their physical appearance, and give a genuine compliment.

For example you could say, "Hey, I know we haven't met but I was standing over there and you just have this amazing energy about you. What's your name?" Or "Hey, I really like the way your hair bounces when you move (smiling). What's your name?" Or "Hey, I just wanted to say that you have an amazing physique. What's your name?"

. . .

From this point, either immediate attraction will be built, or you will immediately get rejected – which is never a big deal, just move on. The more you get rejected or fail at something, the better you will get and the more natural you'll look; and sometimes you did nothing wrong, the other person may have just been having a bad day.

Again, if it successfully opens, you can transition into a story to build more of a connection and establish rapport, since you know the attraction is already there.

Each of these ways to open a conversation is highly variable, and I encourage you to create your own. These were used just so you could get a feel of the 3 different ways to open a conversation. A website with some good examples of openers to start a conversation is: Conversation Starters. Take a look at it if you need some ideas to get started.

TYPES OF STORIES TO TELL

Storytelling for Adults

BEGIN Stories With A Hint or Question

A good way to capture peoples' attention and begin telling a story is by giving a small hint of what is to come. For example, you could start a story with, "Something hilarious happened at work yesterday," or "The craziest thing happened to me yesterday," or "I was so happy this morning."

Also, questions are an excellent way to get a listener tuned in. They get the listener curious about your story. "Have you heard of......?" or "Do you know what happens when you ....?" or "What's the difference between ....?"

After opening or initiating a conversation, a story must follow. There are certain strategies that can be useful depending on whether you want to tell a motivational, funny, or scary story. Adults enjoy hearing stories directed toward what they are facing in life. Below are key tips to telling a variety of types of stories:

How to tell **a motivational story**

Some storytellers are known to be good motivators. You can use your own life story or talk about people you know to deliver an inspiring story. Watch videos on www.youtube.com or www.vimeo.com for examples. When telling a motivational story, include:

- **A story about survival and/or strength.** Tales about near-death experiences and overcoming difficulties are very inspiring because they show human strength. Motivational stories emphasize human mortality, and also reveal how a person can have incredible strength. Use real life experiences to highlight the fact that people can do anything they put their minds to.

- **Be sincere in delivering your message.** Motivational stories are serious and powerful, so there has to be no artifice in the delivery. Try to communicate with a deep level of emotion and sensitivity.

- **Emphasize emotion.** Emotion is what makes a story remarkable and inspirational. The feeling of hope and despair can help people relate to the story better.

How to tell **a funny story**

Funny stories are some of the most popular stories, because they bring laughter and humor into the conversation. Here are some ways you can tell a funny story.

- **Relate embarrassing stories.**
- **Don't try too hard.** It is ironic how a person can be funnier when they are not really trying to be. Also, try too hard and your audience may find it annoying and irrelevant.
- **Keep the story personal.** People tend to respond to people who try to humbly relate their stories. The more honest you are the better.
- **Keep it short.** Short stories tend to be the funniest.
- **Use a particular emotional attitude.** You can choose a particular characteristic or attitude like annoyed or excited and try to live it. You can also sarcastically use the opposite emotion of what you are trying to convey.
- **Don't worry about what other people might say** as you tell your story. Funny stories should sound spontaneous and natural.

How to tell **a scary story**

Even before the birth of horror movies, people already used horror stories to entertain and scare people. The ability to scare people through stories is considered a rare and special talent. Not all storytellers are able to successfully frighten their audience.

- **Voice.** Your voice can be an invaluable tool in telling scary stories. The tone of your voice will make it easier for the audience to feel scared.
- **Do your homework.** Search for the scariest stories you can find and make a list of them. The more realistic they are, the better.
- **Choose new if possible**. Latest stories are a great choice since everyone can relate to it. Urban legends can also work but some of your audience may have already heard the story.
- **Localize it.** Change the setting of the story to make it seem that the story took place in the same place. You can also tie the story to a local resident. Horror stories about a person's locality can have a different impact.
- **Don't over dramatize.** Avoid using words that you do not often use. As a general rule, you have to make it sound like the story makes you uncomfortable inside.
- **Change the setting.** You can change the setting of the story to make it similar to the one you're in. For example, if your town has a local abandoned factory, you can use that as the main setting of your story. Ideally, when your listeners see the factory, they will be reminded of your scary story.

Rapport-Building Stories

People who have gone through tough situations will feel better after talking about it. If you share your tough stories, it may remind the listener of a similar scenario, and he may want to share his stories as well. It is a great way to get people to open up and encourage them to share their own stories. Also, if you can relate to a person's story, and share your own story, that is powerful for creating a connection and building rapport.

An advantage of telling rapport-building stories is that it does make people feel better, and it also forges new friendships. Often, we can be reluctant to share stories because we don't want to be too vulnerable, but once we do, we can enrich the lives of those who hear our stories. It is difficult not to be appreciative of a person after learning their story.

A FEW TIPS For Storytelling To Children

Children love to hear stories. They laugh, smile, giggle, and their ears perk up to the sound of a good story. However, children can also lose attention at the drop of a hat. It can take a lot to capture and maintain their attention.

QUICK FEEDBACK **and its absence**

One of the greatest differences between child and adult audiences is that children give immediate feedback. If they cannot relate to your stories, or if you are not connecting enough with them, they may interrupt you or leave. However, if you do capture their attention, they settle in a comfortable position and look at you with interest. You can use this as a bar to determine how your storytelling is going and what needs to change, if anything.

TONE

Your tone and voice often convey a lot more messages than your words. You may need to change your tone often while dealing with younger children (a higher tone of voice).

The younger the audience is, the more physical your

approach should be. They enjoy you acting the part out, as well as using different accents or tones of voice for different characters in the story.

FINAL TIPS TO BECOMING A MASTER STORYTELLER

A storyteller should always have a clear objective of what they want to say, but at the same time, it's good not to be too focused on it. It's kind of like holding something in the palm of your hand, but not squeezing it tightly. Don't always expect your audience to respond the same way, because then you might not get the response you wanted, and it will show in your face, voice, and body language.

LISTENING

Listening is an important part of storytelling. Although the storyteller does most of the talking, the audience will always find a way to voice what is on their minds. Non-verbal listening, in which the listener displays what they're thinking based on their expressions and gestures, is important for feedback and can give you information on which direction to take the story or continue with what you're saying. If the audience is getting bored, shift the topic of the story or change the tone of your voice to make it sound more exciting.

Probing

Probing is the art of asking the right question at the right time. Throughout the story, you can ask your audience some questions. After relating or telling your story, you can ask your audience about their perceptions and opinions to learn if anything needs to be changed for the next time you tell the story. Do your best to be open-minded and appreciative of what other people are saying, and see it as an opportunity to keep improving your storytelling abilities.

AFTERWORD

I hope you understand how important it is to be a good storyteller, especially in today's world. I encourage you, if you haven't already, to begin creating powerful and memorable stories so you can share them with the world and use them whenever they are needed – whether it be for your family and friends, or people at work, home, in a coffee shop, or anywhere really!